Chaos
to
Control

How. What. Why.
3 Steps to a Cleaner Org

Ian Gotts, Richard Parker, Adrian King

Executive Summary

The phrase "Salesforce@scale Dilemma" was coined by Forrester, the industry analysts. Internal success in an organization breeds demand for more and more. The complexity of scale then crushes Salesforce's responsiveness. As Salesforce use grows, innovation slows, and flexibility evaporates. Why? Every app change risks breaking one of hundreds of data and process customizations, integration links, and third-party add-ons. The Salesforce@scale dilemma is a challenge for customers to overcome, not an inevitable outcome of a Salesforce implementation.

What Admins and Consultants have been searching for is a simple, easily implemented and repeatable approach for cleanup and documentation. It also needs to work for new builds, no matter the size or complexity of Org. And it must be sustainable as the Org evolves.

Where do you start with an Org that has 20,000+ meta data items?

Our HOW. WHAT. WHY. approach is simple, practical and achievable. It takes an operational perspective to help clean up and document an Org. But it is also the approach to keep an Org well documented, so the Salesforce@scale issues do not kick in.

Whilst the approach can be delivered with spreadsheets, the field analysis is massively time consuming, and the config documentation proves almost impossible to maintain.

This is why we've spent the last 3 years building Elements Catalyst. It is an app specifically designed to support Admins and Consultants to deliver Salesforce projects more effectively. It has enterprise scalability and security built in and it is architected to work with the most complex Orgs with multiple Production and Sandboxes. The powerful analysis helps accelerate clean-up efforts and it becomes the central source of all documentation and collaboration for the Org.

A key driver for many organizations is migration to Lightning. This is a significant project which needs careful planning and analysis. The book looks at this specific use case and shows how the approach dovetails with the best practice advice from Salesforce and their experience of migrating their largest internal Org – Org62.

The benefits of moving to Lightning are huge. Salesforce's own research of over 500 companies who had made the switch makes compelling reading; 31% less time managing pipe and 28% less time standardizing processes, with 21% uplift in win rates, 29% faster reporting, 40% improved collaboration, and 41% higher productivity.

Therefore, anything that can accelerate migration must be seriously considered. The first phase of the Lightning Experience Rollout is "Discover" which requires an understanding of what has been configured, a reassessment of business processes to exploit the new Lightning functionality, and a clean-up of the Org.

The approach can deliver tangible savings in this phase. But embedding the good habits means that new Lightning configurations that need to be built to support the migration are well documented. This builds a strong foundation for future enhancements.

The final critical part in the migration is strong change management to drive up user adoption. The existing documentation can be reused as training material, embedded in the new Lightning pages. Any fine tuning to incorporate user feedback is easily implemented.

The approach and Elements Catalyst app provide a very powerful combination to help mitigate the Salesforce@scale Dilemma, so that Salesforce potential is not limited by its own success.

Table of Contents

This book is practical. It is designed to help you get stuff done. And by stuff we mean clean up your Org and get it documented. Every one of you has a different situation, but they seem to fall into some similar use cases which we've laid out in this chapter. If you are looking for a book that will clean up your messy Org with no effort, then walk away now.

You may not want to spend any time understanding why you have a slightly chaotic Org. But this chapter will be useful if you are being questioned by your management about why customizations are taking so long, why changes you make break the Org, or why you are trying to build a business case for a clean-up project. You can read the industry analyst, Forrester's, perspective that they call the Salesforce@scale Dilemma.

For those of you who claim you don't have time for documenting, this chapter is for you. You will recognize some of the challenges that we are seeing from poor documentation: slowed Lightning migrations, maxed out fields on objects and integrations to external systems failing. The worst case is throwing it all away and starting again. The chapter finishes with some horror stories (yes, there are worse Orgs than yours).

HOW. WHAT. WHY. This simple, easily implemented and repeatable approach is what Admins and Consultants have been searching for. The approach works for clean-up and new builds, no matter what size or complexity of Org. And it makes documentation sustainable as the Org evolves. This chapter explains the approach in detail with a worked example.

Elements Catalyst is an affordable app that has been built to help Admins and Consultants clean up, document and build their Orgs. It supports the approach laid out in Chapter 4. This chapter steps you through setting up and configuring Elements Catalyst.

This chapter explores the powerful analysis and documentation capabilities of Elements Catalyst and shows how to apply them to the HOW. WHAT. WHY. approach. This may be the first time you have seen a perspective of your Org like this. Understanding how to use the detailed field analysis will eliminate man hours of tedious work. It also shows the best way to add documentation and collaborate with your team.

To keep your Org documented requires a change in habits. This chapter explores ways to engrain those habits, and how Elements Catalyst supports you.

For many of you the Lightning Migration is what has forced you to look at the Org, clean up and document it. This chapter draws on Salesforce best practice on how to migrate to Lightning, including the case study of their own internal migration of Org62. It then shows how Elements Catalyst can help accelerate not only the clean-up but also the adoption.

There is a great book written by Accenture called "The Director's Cut". It draws parallels between movies and software implementations. How do movie directors create new value with their previously released films? They issue a "director's cut"— a revised, updated version of a previously released movie over which the director has complete artistic control.

Chapter 10: Keeping on top of your Org   85

Arguably the more important process is the process of process improvement. How do you constantly evolve and enhance Salesforce without getting yourself back in the same hole: an undocumented Org that is slowing innovation. We have built a process map called the Salesforce Development Lifecycle which anyone can download and tailor.

Appendix 1: Resources and Links   87

Here are useful resources including links to everything that was referenced in the book.

Appendix 2: Running Live Workshops   89

Over the last 20 years, we've run 1,000's of live workshops. The way we think about them, prepare for them, deliver them is described in detail in this appendix.

Authors

IAN GOTTS

Founder and CEO

Elements.cloud

ian@elements.cloud

@iangotts

CEO and founder of Elements.cloud based in Salesforce Tower, San Francisco, but can be found speaking at User Groups, World Tours and Dreamforce – or in an airport lounge practicing his bass guitar.

Prior to Elements.cloud he was co-founder and CEO of Nimbus - a Salesforce customer from 2001 - which was acquired by TIBCO in 2011. The Nimbus business analysis app was used by 1000+ clients including Nestle, HSBC, SAP, Barclays, Toyota, Sara Lee, AstraZeneca, non-profits and Government.

Prior to that he was CIO of the largest UK Government agency, and an Associate Partner at Accenture where he led the Program Management practice.

He is an author of 10 books, a prolific blogger with a rare ability to make the complex seem simple which makes him a sought after and entertaining conference speaker. And he is powered by Duracell.

RICHARD PARKER
Founder and CCO
Elements.cloud
richard@elements.cloud
@RP_Elements

Co-founder of Nimbus and key to the development of the product and approach. He led Sales and Consulting globally with some of the largest enterprises in the world, including Nestlé, Orange, Chevron, AstraZeneca, Novartis, Toyota and Central Government.

Richard is an author of Common Approach, Uncommon Results and is an experienced conference speaker.

Living in France on Lake Annecy he'll be found on the water in the summer and slopes in the winter.

ADRIAN KING
Founder and CIO & CTO
Elements.cloud
adrian@elements.cloud

An experienced software entrepreneur, with a background in R&D and strong operational experience in global software firms.

He was CIO and COO of Nimbus, and prior to that was responsible for R&D at a series of global software firms. He was also turnaround CEO of a startup in the oil and gas drilling space where he redefined their product strategy based on the buying culture of their target market.

He provides strategy consulting to a number of businesses with an emphasis on leveraging IT and optimizing operations.

An avid cyclist, when he's not working, he's road or mountain biking around the Hampshire, UK countryside.

Chapter 1: Is this book for you?

This book is designed to help you get stuff done. It is not clever prose or abstract theory. It is 'roll your sleeves up', practical, achievable actions. But you need to read the book through your own lens. What challenges are you facing? What do you need to get delivered? Read this chapter to find a use case (or three) that matches where you are.

If some of the use cases kinda-fit, but not quite, then talk to us. If you are looking for a "push a button and my Org is fully documented" answer, forget it. It doesn't exist. You'll need to do some work. We're just trying to do as much as we can for you.

This book sets out an approach that could be implemented using spreadsheets and slides. But we've been told by customer after customer that this is a nightmare and completely unsustainable.

Which is why Chapter 5 explains how the Elements Catalyst app can help you clean up, document and build your Org with less pain. It was designed to support the approach and the uses cases.

Just about to leave a company and as I was about to walk out of the door they said,
'Hey Davina could you give us some documentation on what you've been doing the last 5 years.'

Davina Hanchuck, Manager, CRM Systems at Instructure

USE CASE 01: You are migrating to Lightning

You've run the Lightning Experience Readiness report and are taking a phased approach. It is clear you cannot simply "switch it on" as there are changes to be made. But you want to get the benefits of the cool Lightning features. You need to work through all the items that need fixing and then decide how your users' experience could be transformed. That means changes to page layouts, validation rules, workflow and more. Getting a grip on how and why these customizations were made is a vital first step.

This project may seem daunting. You take one look at your Org and it's like unknotting a huge mess of ropes. You tug one loose end, and everything seems to move, and the knot gets tighter. Where do you even start?

Using the Lightning Experience Readiness report and Elements Catalyst Org analytics, you can see where to focus your clean-up efforts to get some quick wins. You can draw quick process diagrams to understand the flow. As you build your new Lightning experience, you have a place to start documenting what and why. The trick is to make this documentation approach a habit. Then the impact assessment of future changes becomes so much easier.

USE CASE 02: Building new Org

You are building a new Org and want to avoid the documentation horror stories you've heard before. If you are looking for a practical and sustainable way of documenting your Org configurations as you go, while it's fresh in your mind, then this is for you.

Now you have an opportunity to take a process-led approach to the implementation and get a better understanding of your users' requirements, so you build what they need, not what they thought they wanted. Think about how you are going to configure Salesforce from an end-to-end process perspective: lead to order, quote to cash, inquiry to resolution. You can then tie the processes, the thinking behind the changes, and the specifications back to the customizations you make to Salesforce. The trick is to make this documentation approach a habit. Then the impact assessment of future changes becomes so much easier.

USE CASE 03: Enhancing an existing Org

You have a new project that is building on previous configurations. You need an approach for documenting what was built before - and why - so you can understand what to clean up and delete. Next you have to find way of maintaining it with the planned changes that you will be making. You want to leave the Org in a better state than you found it.

Resist the urge to just jump in and start more customizations. Using Elements Catalyst Org analytics, you can focus on the area that you are changing and start to see the scale of the problem and the configuration connections. You may also get some clean-up quick wins. Then you have a place to start documenting what you've discovered and tag items that can be deleted. This means you can clean up the Org as you go. Once you make this documentation approach a habit, you build a great picture of your configuration and the impact assessment of future changes becomes so much easier.

USE CASE 04: Running a "clean-up Org" project

You and your team have recognized that the lack of documentation is holding back future development. You have funding for a project to document your Org(s). You are looking for a proven approach and tools to support you. Plus, you want to put in place an approach that keeps the Org documented.

This project may seem daunting. You take one look at your Org and it's like unknotting a huge mess of ropes or those power cables behind your desk. You tug on one loose end and the knot gets tighter. Where do you even start? Using Element Catalyst Org analytics, you can see where to focus your clean-up efforts to get some quick wins. Then you have a place to start documenting what you've discovered and tag those items that can be deleted. Making this documentation approach a habit is the trick. Then the impact assessment of future changes becomes so much easier.

USE CASE 05: Trying to get back under control

You are tasked with implementing new capabilities, but the lack of documentation is holding back future development. There is tension between getting an understanding of what was built and documenting it - and the desire to "just get on with" implementing new features. You are looking for an efficient and proven approach and tools to support you in getting stakeholders on the same page to understand the impact of what's been done to date – and decisions that need to be made to move forward with the current work.

Your Org looks and feels like a large plate of spaghetti. You haven't the time or budget to run a clean-up project. Using Elements Catalyst Org analytics, you can focus on the area of the Org you are changing and start to see the scale of the problem and the configuration connections. Then you have a place to start documenting what you've discovered and tag those items that can be deleted. You can clean up the Org as you go, getting some quick wins along the way. Once you start documenting, every future change will be easier.

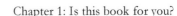

USE CASE 06: New admin trying to understand what you have inherited

You have inherited an Org and need to quickly understand what you've let yourself in for. You are under pressure to deliver a raft of changes, but before you do that you need to get a handle on what was configured before you arrived. Only then can you give any realistic estimates for the changes people are expecting you to deliver.

Elements Catalyst Org analytics will give a you a full picture of the Org so you can understand the risk of changes that are being suggested. You can focus on specific areas of the Org you are changing, see the scale of the problem and the configuration connections. Then you have a place to start documenting what you've discovered and tag those items that can be deleted. This is a critical part of cleaning up your Org. You may discover some quick wins as you go. You need to strive to make this documentation approach a habit because then the assessment of future changes and their impact becomes so much easier.

USE CASE 07: Consultant starting a new project

You have started a project on an Org and need to quickly understand all of its functionality and configuration. And of course, you're under pressure to deliver the project quickly. You need to be able to give realistic estimates for all project deliverables and know the risks.

Elements Catalyst Org analytics will give you a complete model of the Org so you can understand every component of the Org, how much it is being used, and who is using it. You'll be able to estimate timescales and risk for the project. It will also give you a framework for gathering requirements and user stories, building business processes, and leaving the client with a fully documented Org. If you involve and engage the client in the whole business analysis lifecycle, you have a better chance of getting them to make the documentation approach a habit.

USE CASE 08: Consultant with clean-up project

The client has decided that this is best done by you, and there are high expectations as this is probably seen as a costly project diverting effort from that backlog of changes. They also want recommendations on tools and approach to keep the Org documented. Ideally, you want to leave the Org in a better state than you found it.

You take one look at the Org and it's as scary as a pit full of snakes. Where do you even start? Using Elements Catalyst Org Analytics, you get a clear view of configuration, usage and impact. You'll almost certainly see some quick wins to give the client confidence. You also have a structured place to start documenting what you've discovered and tag those items that can be deleted. By engaging the client, you have a better chance of getting them to make the documentation approach a habit.

Chapter 1: Is this book for you?

Chapter 2: Why does no one have a well-documented Org?

You **may NOT want to spend any time understanding why you have a slightly chaotic Org**. If that's the case, then skip this chapter.

This chapter will be useful if:

- You are being questioned why customizations are taking so long or why changes break the Org
- You are trying to build a business case and plan for a clean-up project or Lightning migration
- You are just interested in the evolution of Salesforce; tactical to strategic
- You want to hear that you are not alone!!

Salesforce has gone from tactical to strategic

When we started using Salesforce back in 2001, it was easy. It was a basic SFA (Salesforce automation) with Accounts, Contacts and Leads. I don't think Opportunity had been launched. The potential of CRM in the cloud was huge. Then the powerful configuration capabilities of Force.com was launched to turn Salesforce into a platform – which was a game changer.

The potential of a customizable app in the cloud was massive. But the scope of most implementations was limited – SFA. We were pretty unusual as we decided to run the whole company on Salesforce.

Chapter 2: Why does no one have a well-documented Org?

We built 250 objects to support procurement, HR, compliance, change projects, IT & hosting. The AppExchange didn't exist, so we had to build it all ourselves. When FinancialForce launched their accounting app on the platform, we were an early customer. The power of one connected app all on the same platform to manage the business was immense.

Roll the clock forward 18 years and Salesforce is becoming strategic in organization after organization. Why? The string of acquisitions, the ecosystem of AppExchange apps and the ability to build complex apps with clicks not code, means that Salesforce can support a huge range of operations. No longer is it just sales teams. In fact, in 2018, the number of companies investing $20m per year with Salesforce doubled, and those spending over $1 million per year was up 43%.

It really comes back to the strategic relationships that we're driving with these customers: they're deeper and more meaningful.

Keith Block, Co-CEO of Salesforce

When Salesforce was tactical and had a narrow scope, developing with limited or no documentation was (probably) acceptable. It was not recommended, but it was the norm. But to have a strategic app that is critical to the ongoing operation of the organization with no documentation is probably negligent. It certainly puts the organization at huge risk.

Every Org is constantly evolving. This can be incremental changes to tweak and improve the user experience, all the way up to major change projects to implement new functionality, such as Lightning, CPQ or Einstein. All these changes need to build on the existing Org. To do this with any level of confidence requires decent documentation of what has been built before. An implementation with no clear documentation of what has been configured – and (most importantly) why - means that it is very difficult, if not impossible, to support, maintain and improve.

The Salesforce@scale dilemma – Forrester Report

"Clients are impressed by Salesforce's CRM applications, which are more modern and user-pleasing than older applications. And they love Force.com's high productivity for developers to configure the CRM applications as well as create new applications from scratch.

Initial success breeds demand for more and more. As additional departments ask for Salesforce subscriptions, business leaders want to expand initial wins with Salesforce CRM into customer and/or partner engagement, marketing automation and analytics. New custom applications and customizations mushroom.

In addition, the complexity of scale crushes Salesforce's responsiveness. As Salesforce use grows, innovation slows, and flexibility evaporates.

Why? Every app change risks breaking one of hundreds of data and process customizations, integration links, and third-party add-ons.

The result: every change requires long and expensive impact-analysis and regression testing projects – killing the responsiveness that made Salesforce attractive at the start.

The Salesforce@scale dilemma is a challenge for clients to overcome, rather than an inevitable outcome of large-scale, strategic Salesforce implementations. It is a big issue because Salesforce has become a much more strategic supplier in technology strategies to win, serve and retain customers."

John R. Rymer, Computer Weekly

FORRESTER   Industry Analyst Report May 2017[1]
Five ways to cut the risk of Salesforce

---

[1] Report summary
https://www.computerweekly.com/feature/Five-ways-to-cut-the-risk-of-Salesforce

Lightning Experience amplifies the problems

Lightning Experience gives ultimate configurability. Lightning pages are now super sexy with dynamic components. Data from multiple objects can be dropped onto a single page using standard or 3rd party components. Pages can be designed to support every use case. An Admin walking into another organization could look at their Salesforce Org and not even recognize it.

This is why it is even more important to document why you have configured things as you have. Your Lightning migration project is the perfect time to start the documentation habit.

An example of this is Kimble - the Professional Services Automation app. It is available on the AppExchange. All the configuration and customization are performed through custom pages and stored in custom objects that Kimble have developed. The Admin doesn't ever go into Setup. In fact, some customers don't even realize that the app is running on Salesforce.

Documentation debt kills agility, slows innovation & wastes time

Technical debt is a concept in software development that reflects the implied cost of additional rework caused by choosing an easy solution now instead of using a better approach that would take longer. Short term gain, long term pain.

The issue we are all facing is documentation debt. We make changes to an area of the Org but don't take the time to document what and why. We just need to get it out. But we come back 6 months, 6 weeks or 6 days[2] later and want to make further changes to the same area. But we can't remember what was done so it takes hours of investigative work – this is Documentation debt.

Documentation debt has a real impact. One of the reasons for Salesforce's huge success is that it is so easy to configure using drag and drop. It doesn't require lots of coding. But documentation debt kills that agility.

Even the simplest change could potentially impact different areas of the business. Currently, one option is to look in Salesforce Setup and do a ton of detective work[3]. There are so many configuration options that the risk is that you could miss something, break the Org and stop the business operating. Another option is to create new customizations rather than change the existing ones. This bloats the Org with multiple similar objects, fields, flows and validation rules, process builder workflows, etc.

---

[2] In my case 6 hours #seniormoment
[3] Or you could try deleting it and see if you get errors, or someone in the company shouts.

Chapter 3: Documentation is an accelerator

"Documenting stuff takes time which could be spent developing more stuff the users want."

You need to change that mindset.

Spend to Save. 2 steps back to take 3 forward. Paying forward.

Call it what you want, but deep down you know that you should be documenting what you are customizing as you are doing it. If your Salesforce implementation is strategic, then making changes without any documentation could be considered negligent.

What is stopping you?

- **We don't have the time:** you know that doing it will save time in the long run. You need to plan time into the project
- **Consultants are doing it:** you need to be clear in your SOW what you need them to do which supports the Org long term
- **Our developers are doing it:** probably not, and you need to agree this with them
- **No systematic, sustainable approach:** this is the key issue

This last point is fundamental. There has been no solution that ties the documentation back to the customizations that is EASY and SUSTAINABLE. Until now. That is what this book is about.

The following issues, that could all be solved with a clear view of everything in the Org, are what we are seeing and hearing from our Salesforce network and customers.

Migrating to Lightning

Everyone wants to be on Lightning. The UI is engaging. All the new productivity enhancing features are in Lightning. And Salesforce's investments are in Lightning.

Migration to Lightning gives you an opportunity to simplify and optimize your Org. With the new features you can rethink operational processes and get the huge benefits you see other customers talking about. You can eliminate page layouts by combining them using dynamic Lightning components. Managed packages that were installed but rarely used can be deleted, and work-arounds can be found for managed packages that are not yet Lightning ready[4]. Finally, the Lightning Migration Readiness report has probably identified that there are customizations that need to be changed to make Lightning work.

All this raises the ugly question. "How does our Org work?" It is difficult to optimize and simplify if your view of the business processes and related customizations is hazy. The risk is that making changes could have unforeseen results. The worst-case scenario is that the Org stops working.

We just did a study of 500+ Salesforce customers who made the move to Lightning, and they saw an average 41% increase in productivity

Lightning Experience, Readiness Check Overview[5]

---

[4] Yes there are ISVs still not Lightning Ready. Guys – get with the program!!
[5] Lightning Readiness Check Overview *https://sforce.co/2D3rf8W*

Cannot continue development – maxed out fields

The ecosystem is rife with stories of Orgs with objects that maxed out the fields. Normally it is Account, Contact, Lead and Opportunity. The sad fact is that many of these additional fields are no longer used but were never deleted.

Also, ISV managed packages often add custom fields to the standard objects in addition to all the custom objects that they install. Deleting fields is often the bulk of the clean-up activities. But of course, you daren't delete a field if you don't know where or if it is used. There is the classic "I just need to find 10 fields I can delete to deliver this project or install this managed package.

This bloating can reach a hiatus. Objects are maxed out, so no new fields can be added without upgrading the entire Org to the next edition level – a huge, unnecessary cost. And there are Ultimate Edition Orgs that have maxed out their fields so have nowhere to go. Yes, seriously.

We heard of a client who had maxed out the fields on Task object. That is 500 custom fields! Pause for a moment to let that sink in.

Critical integrations to Salesforce being broken

Salesforce is not an island. In most large organizations, particularly those where it has evolved into a strategic platform, Salesforce has integrations with other systems. But it is often not clear how those integrations work. They may use custom fields that hold temporary data, so at first glance, the fields don't seem to be used, have no data, are not on page layouts, reports or email templates. So, it appears they can be deleted.

Perhaps the integration relies on validation rules or process-builder to make sure the data is clean. Someone must have thought it through and written a spec. Figuring that out is often trial and error, or firefighting the results of the integration failing.

This is a huge risk.

How and why you built that integration is gold dust. As you try to understand how it works, capture the information as process diagrams, notes and whiteboard sketches, and store them alongside all the customizations that are involved. That same bit of documentation may be linked to multiple customizations: object, fields, Apex trigger, validation rule…

I love the excitement of deleting a field and waiting for the screams

Said no-one…EVER

Cost of poor documentation

We are hearing about more and more projects where the sole aim is to document what has been configured and clean up the Org. These projects need a structured approach for recording what they discover and an impact analysis so that items can be deleted with confidence.

Some of these projects are being awarded to consulting firms, which means this is not a low-cost exercise. The thinking is probably, "the consultants made this mess, they must be able to figure out what they did". But the consultants have been on 10 projects since they last worked on your Org. They are as clueless as you are about why you used that email template combined with those validation rules and process builder workflow. The ROI for embedding better documentation approach and habits from the start is clear. And unless you have a rigorous approach to documenting what you or they find, you will be in the same position six months from now.

Some Orgs are so complex and poorly documented that they are impossible to develop further. Or the consolidation of multiple Orgs is proving impossible. In these situations, customers are deciding to throw away the Org and start again, with all the costs of configuration and implementation. They have determined that is the easiest, lowest risk and cheapest approach. Right there is another solid business case for good documentation: the cost of a new implementation.

10 Org horror stories

Don't worry, there is someone out there who has a bigger nightmare than you. Here are few stories we've heard when talking to the ecosystem.

- 500 fields on Task object
- 60,000 metadata items and 48,000 field usage records
- 15,000 reports
- 49,700 email templates (long story)
- 464 fields (all used) and 14 stages on Opportunity object
- 800 fields maxed out Contact Object consolidating 5 orgs
- 100+ picklist values on a field, no idea which are used
- 55 Orgs and trying to consolidate
- 5372 Apex Classes and 55 Managed Packages
- 1,500,000 lines of undocumented Apex code

There are more of these at *elements.cloud/confessions*

Chapter 4: A health plan for your Org

"I know my Org's sick. But how bad is it, Doc?"

The Lightning Migration Readiness Report and Salesforce Optimizer are great tools that any Admin can run. But like your annual medical checkup, they give you an overall view of the health of your Org. They do not get into the nitty gritty detail that you need to plan and execute your clean-up or documentation efforts.

What Admins and Consultants have been searching for is a simple, easily implemented and repeatable approach. The approach needs to work for clean-up and also new builds, no matter what size or complexity of Org. And it must be sustainable as the Org evolves.

Where do you start with an Org that has 20,000+

meta data items?

This is why we wrote this book.

An operational perspective

Where do you start? It is not realistic to look at your growing Org and try to work out what everything does and document it. Most of the customizations are probably no longer used. You want to find out what is being used.

Just focusing on one area – e.g. all Apex triggers or all Process Builder Workflows – is also challenging as the customizations are so interconnected. You cannot look at an Apex Trigger in isolation from the business process it supports. Like unknotting a ball of wool; pull on one thread and the knot just gets tighter.

The best approach is to come at your clean-up efforts from an operational perspective. Think of an object and focus on how it works. For example, the Opportunity object.

What is the lifecycle of an opportunity, from raised to closed? Document that as a process diagram and find all the customizations related to making it work. Then take another area, "the lifecycle of a case" and document that.

Every Org is different, but this approach can be applied to all of them. For many, the starting point will be the 5 key standard objects – Lead, Account, Contact, Opportunity and Case. But for some that have implemented an 'industry" Managed Package (e.g. NPSP, HEDA, Health, Financial Services, Telco etc.) it may be a different starting point. But the same approach.

Firefighting vs strategy

We realize that some of you may be in firefighting mode so you will need to take a very tactical approach rather than the more strategic operational approach. Some examples of firefighting are:

- This Apex trigger is failing. Why?
- We've run out of fields on Case and we need to find at least 10 we can delete without breaking anything
- An app that is integrated to Salesforce is being upgraded and we need to understand what fields, validation rules and workflows are used for the integration so that we can check it will still work

Steady, measurable progress

The benefit of an operational approach is you can make steady, achievable progress. It's just like going to the gym. If you were told on Day 1 that you had to do 100 pushups and 50 pull ups you'd never get started. Instead, you start small and increase little by little. Six months later you will be staggered by how far you have come. You may start with Opportunity object, but fairly soon you have documented all the key objects that run your business[6].

This simple, achievable, "chipping away" approach is a great way of documenting your Org.

---

[6] . It is more important to build regular habits, rather than be a "weekend hero". This simple 7 min exercise routine is easy and works. Even when travelling a lot. *https://7-min.com/*

Tracking progress and showing your value

Often, as a Salesforce Admin you are the unsung hero battling your way through an unstoppable barrage of change requests and the constant waves of new Salesforce releases. And don't forget the changes that the ISVs are making to their managed packages and pushing them into your Org.

The danger is that a clean-up exercise goes unnoticed. Or worse, what is noticed is that you aren't adding more features requests from the backlog.

The question, "What did you accomplish this week?" is often difficult to answer – even if it is only your inner voice doubting you on Friday evening. But, in the same way my FitBit keeps a record of physical progress[7], Elements Catalyst keeps track of documentation progress.

Remember you might need to take 2 steps back to take 3 leaps forward. The following section describes the straightforward and effective way you can document/clean up your Org, that also tracks your progress and shows value.

---

[7] And there's no doubt it both nags and motivates. I refused to take any buses, taxis or escalators during Dreamforce!

HOW. WHAT. WHY.

We have a simple 3-step approach that is practical, achievable and helps you make measurable progress.

1. **HOW**: How does this part of the Org/business work?

2. **WHAT**: What did you change in Salesforce to support it?

3. **WHY**: Why were changes made and where is the documentation that describes why and how you changed Salesforce?

HOW DOES IT WORK?   **WHAT** DID YOU CHANGE?   **WHY** WE DID WE DO IT?

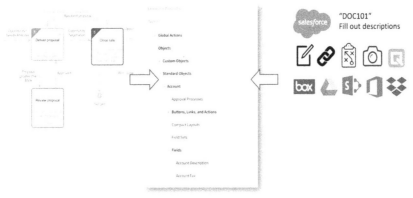

We think our 3 step HOW. WHAT. WHY. approach is best described by a simple process flow[8], which is shown below. You can see it is a couple of nested loops, but don't get freaked out. It is all very straightforward. Next, we'll show how it works in practice.

Pick a discrete area

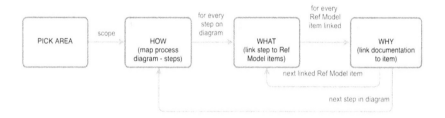

Take a small area that's relevant to the work you are doing. You probably have a very clear view of your top 3 hit list. Here are some examples that we hear about from customers:

- To migrate to Lightning we need to understand how to simplify page layouts, validation rules and automation, and fix the migration issues
- Users are complaining about slow page loads and busy page layouts, so we need to look at that Object and how to reduce the fields on the page layouts
- We've reached field limits on Objects so need to work out which we can delete
- So many of the reports have never been used. Which ones can we delete?
- We are working through all the Apex triggers trying to understand their interactions and if they are all used
- There are multiple process builder workflows that all seem to do the same thing

---

[8] With only 4 boxes!!!

Alternatively, you can use the Elements Catalyst Org Analytics report to help you identify where to focus. It shows you which Objects are least well documented4, the number of custom fields by object, and gives each field an impact rating.

The trick is to keep the scope tight and small. You need to make measurable and visible progress, especially for your first project when all eyes are on you.

HOW - does it work?

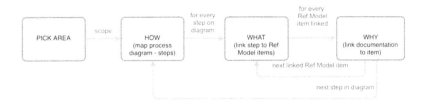

HOW is all about understanding how the business operates and is best described as a simple process diagram. It is how the users use Salesforce to get their job done. It is how that automation or integration works behind the scenes.

Process diagrams are valuable assets and have 3 audiences. They have a life beyond the project:

- **Admins, Business Analysts and Developers:** for app development
- **End Users:** training material to drive up adoption
- **Auditors:** for regulated industries process diagrams are the evidence that you are "saying what you do and doing what you say"

Mapping business processes & notation

Mapping processes can feel daunting, especially when you start talking to IT teams who often use a complex modelling notation. For business process mapping we recommend a simple notation that has been proven in 1,000's of projects over the last 20 years.

Diagrams can be drawn in any format or style, but this approach really works:

- Draw the diagrams in a simple left to right process flow aiming to have no more than 8-10 process steps per diagram, called activity boxes.
- The activity box is a single, simple building block to show what is done and by whom. It is all you need. You don't need lots of different shapes. Trust us.
- You MUST have lines between boxes with text. These define the handoffs, which is where most processes break down. The more specific the better.
- Any activity box can have lower level "child diagrams". This makes each diagram simple, with the detail in lower levels.
- Think about the 3 audiences when creating these diagrams: admin/developers, end users, compliance/auditors.

In this video our wonderful colleague Walter will explain some of the principles. You can watch the 9 minutes now and see how it's done.

VIDEO LINK *http://bit.ly/processmapping*

If you didn't watch the video, read from here......

Process mapping notation

The cool thing about this notation is that there is only ONE shape to worry about. You can describe any process, no matter how complex, in a way that everyone understands - without any training.

So, the way of thinking about a process diagram is this: what happens in terms of actions (verb and noun) which together produce the desired outcome.

Why do we start it and why do we complete it (input/output)? Who carries these steps out (role/resource) - can be human or system.

How is each step carried out in detail (drill down to lower level child diagram - blue corner) or link to supporting documentation (paperclip)?

Hints on designing process diagrams:

- **Input/output:** The lines between activity boxes show the triggers and outcomes. Every activity box must have lines connecting them. And every line must have line text. If the activity is "Process Invoice" then try to avoid calling the output "processed invoice" but instead try to be more specific. Is it "approved invoice" or "validated invoice"?

- **What happens:** It starts with a verb: Create email, Raise opportunity, Triage and route case, Assign task, Win order, Onboard team member. Try to avoid the words "manage" or "process". Get more specific.

- **Resource:** One or more resources can be attached to an activity box. They describe who is responsible for an activity e.g. Salesforce Admin, Customer Success Manager, but can also be a system e.g. Salesforce, Pardot. They are an alternative to swimlanes and keep the diagrams tighter.

- **Drill down corner:** The corner shows that this activity has a lower level diagram. You can drill down as many levels as you need to keep each diagram simple.

- **Links:** The paperclip shows that there are links to attachments – notes, images, URL links. Get creative. Does the step need a supporting document, screenshot or training video?

The Opportunity process diagram

Here is a process diagram that describes the simplistic lifecycle of an opportunity. It's actually a drill down from the top (organizational) level diagram. You can see that each step also has drill downs to lower level diagrams. There is no limit to the number of levels that you can drill down.

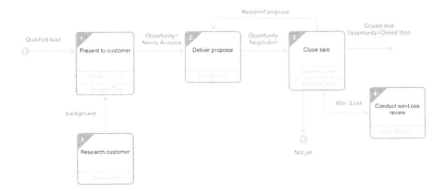

Imagine creating this diagram in a workshop setting with all stakeholders[9]. You might discover it's not the process that everyone follows or believes happens. The power of a mapping workshop is getting shared agreement, then communicating that process to everyone to get adoption.

You will also probably identify some quick wins. This happens when people start seeing the process and the handoffs between the steps.

Don't be scared if the diagram becomes large with 20+ activities. Later you can simplify by taking a group of activity boxes and "sending to child" which means creating a lower level diagram.

---

[9] We can all dream

Sometimes, where the process is well understood but not documented, this is really quick to do. In other cases, documenting the process highlights the fact that there is some disagreement how the process works (or should work) – and it takes a slightly longer. But don't underestimate the value of this mapping.

We've got years of experience process mapping. Getting everyone on the same page – literally – is so empowering.

I managed a team who mapped out the project processes for a construction company. At the end of the work we identified a ROI across the company's major construction projects of $198,000 – PER DAY!!!! One of their long serving VPs said that the process mapping workshops were the most rewarding work he had done in his 30-year career. High praise indeed.

A 4-hour workshop consolidated 40 processes into ONE, which saves us 40 hours of work EVERY WEEK.[10]

David Limiero, Stadia Church Planting

The simple notation explained

A simple notation is required to be able to develop a process map that every employee, partner or supplier can understand, no matter what their background, level of seniority, or discipline. The principles were first published in a book called Common Approach UnCommon Results, which we wrote in 2004. The notation was published in 2008 as an open standard called UPN (Universal Process Notation). We have simplified UPN even more, based on client experience.

UPN has been proven by 1000s of companies in every industry from highly regulated Fortune 500 companies down to nimble startups. It works. This simple notation has been designed to make understanding processes easy for everyone: end users, IT, compliance, consultants and executives.

WHAT – do you use in Salesforce?

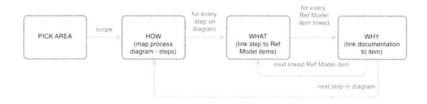

Now you work your way through the process diagram step-by-step and ask the question "What in Salesforce do we use to deliver this step?"

This could be an object, field, page layout, email template, process builder workflow etc.

Don't be surprised when you find the same items are linked to a number of different process steps and are used by different departments. This is where documentation becomes a critical resource for impact analysis for any new changes.

There is no "right and wrong" here, but decide on an approach and be consistent to help people leverage this. Some people link the highest levels of their process map to the Objects involved.

Then on the detailed lower level diagrams, process steps may have links to validation rules, specific triggers, or a detailed automated activity that was created in Process Builder or Flow.

Looking at the process diagram below, process step 1 "Present to customer" is linked to the Opportunity, Account and Contact objects and maybe some custom objects that support this process step.

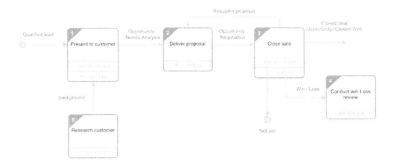

If we were to drill down to the lower level diagram below box 1, we could start to attach other customizations.

You will bump into all sorts of things en-route which are not related to what you are doing, and you may want to add a quick note or a tag to them.

Adding tags means you can report on items later, filter and sort. Tags could be "Release36", "delete" or "reviewed". If you use tags to identify which items are used by which departments, you could use them to identify training needs. Tagging will also help you understand the conflicts in changes to any item.

WHY – did you do it that way?

Often the most valuable documentation is the Why. What was the thinking behind the configuration and why was it configured in that way?

As you start linking items in the Org Model to the process steps, look for anything that was created that describes why changes were made and what was updated: requirements, user stories, process sketches, ERD/data models, videos, specifications, screenshots, wire diagrams, photo of whiteboards, notes, audio clips from the developer.

The mantra is, "*if you created it, link it*".

We know this is hard, so we are working on ways to make it feel easier and more immediate - like our mobile app[11]. You can take a photo when you are in the meeting and post it straight to the item in the Org Model, or create a note using Siri. Just like we all do with social media.

Also, our Chrome Extension[12] means you can access analysis and documentation held in Elements Catalyst, but from inside Salesforce Setup.

---

[11] Search for Elements Catalyst in the App Store from your phone
[12] Download from the Google Chrome Store *http://bit.ly/insidesalesforce*

A single view of all configuration knowledge

Documentation describes how and why you made those changes and is in a huge range of formats: specifications, notes, photos of whiteboards, screenshots, data models/ERD, URL links to wikis, apps and files in cloud storage, wireframe designs, process diagrams, requirements and user stories…and the list goes on. What is really powerful, is when all of that documentation can be seen in the context of the Org configurations.

The issue is that these are probably all sitting in different file stores and there is no context or relationship between them. There was a relationship in the mind of the project team when they were created, but that has gone. Forever.

Give these different documents context and a home by linking them to the Org metadata items that they relate to. Then you will build up a picture of what has been built and why, so that impact analysis of future changes becomes easier.

Elements can enable "future you" to remember why "current you" made a design / process decision for good reasons.

Kristi Guzman, Senior Salesforce Administrator, ACN MVP, DF18 speaker

Often people document the "what". What is the object? What is this record type? What does the flow do? That's great, but even long after all that created, you can go back and work out what it is. Really you want to capture the thinking behind why it was done that way.

Salesforce is so powerful there are often several ways of meeting a user's requirement. Sometimes there are horrible workarounds using clicks not code, but several releases later - that functionality is in the core platform. You look at customizations, not realizing when they were made and the platform limitations at the time, and say, "Why did you do it that way?"

The other reason for quirky customizations is a lack of platform knowledge by the Admin or the consultant doing the work.

The final reason is the "I don't have time to do it properly. I'll hack it and come back and fix it later," and "later" never comes.

Linking the documentation to multiple places

There is a many-to-many relationship between customizations and documentation. A document may need to be linked to all the customized items it impacted: new email template, a new object or fields with validation rules, a process builder workflow, updated page layouts, and new permission sets. And any item might be customized to support different use cases, so will have many different documents attached.

There are different types of "documentation", so don't just think about textual documents.

Notes: Documentation can just be notes. You discovered something about how this item was configured or why and you want a place to record it. Quickly add a note, bearing in mind that a note is tied to a single item in the Org Model.

Documentation in cloud storage:[13] Documentation can be stored anywhere - GoogleDrive, Box, Sharepoint, GitHub, wikis, webpages. As mentioned earlier, it can be anything stored there.

If the links are stored in a central URL Links library, it will be easier to attached any URL link to multiple places. And if the URL destination moves you only have one place to change it - in the library. Everywhere that references it, is immediately up-to-date. This is really important if you are linking to screens in Salesforce and you are moved from one instance to another e.g. NA32 to NA69 or you implement My Domain and then rebrand.

Process diagrams and data models/ERD: Ideally, process and data models can be drawn in Elements Catalyst (we covered this in the WHAT section). But they could also be PDFs of Visio, PowerPoint, Draw.io, Lucidchart or photos of whiteboards stored in the cloud. It doesn't matter what the format is.

What does matter is that the diagrams were drawn because a process or data model is the easiest way to capture what the app needs to do – unambiguously. Arguably it is the FIRST thing you should be doing before you jump into customizing Salesforce.[14]

---

[13] People say they have NO documentation. But there is often some hanging around.
[14] IMHO ADM201, Trailhead and implementation training don't emphasize the importance of business analysis. Don't get me started!!!

Images: Add a screenshot or photo of a whiteboard. These are compressed and stored against an Org Model item. If you want to link to multiple items - either save in cloud storage and use URL link (as above) or just attach multiple places.

Additional metadata: There may be structured data you want to capture in a form so that you can report on it. For example, the effort, risk and timing to migrate to Lightning.

Integrations to other apps: Is this item used in an integration to an app that is outside Salesforce core platform. This could be Salesforce Pardot or 3rd party apps like Workday, SAP or Oracle.

Simple. Practical. Achievable.

You've now seen our simple 3-step approach. The power is that it can be done as a dedicated project or as a part time activity alongside other development work. And you can make the scope of the clean-up exercise pretty small and tight so that you can show measurable progress.

In summary

1. **HOW:** How does this part of the Org/business work?

2. **WHAT:** What did you change in Salesforce to support it?

3. **WHY:** Why were changes made and where is the documentation that describes why and how you changed Salesforce?

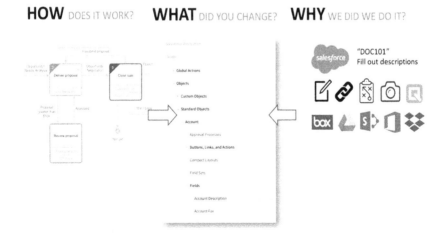

Chapter 4: A health plan for your Org

Chapter 5: Elements Catalyst

As we said earlier, you could manage all this configuration documentation in a set of spreadsheets and then try and keep them up-to-date as your Org evolves. But this is mind-bogglingly difficult, especially if you have development work going on in multiple sandboxes.

What is really required is an app designed to do the job properly, which can also add a ton of insights to help your clean-up exercises.

Which is why we've spent the last 3 years building Elements Catalyst

Elements Catalyst combines multiple elements (ahem) in a secure, scalable and affordable enterprise app.

At the center is the Org Model (a synchronized copy of all your Org metadata) that can be linked to process diagrams, data models, documentation, requirements and user stories.

There are no apps out there that even come close to its functionalities.

Kelsey Shannon, CRM Manager. Honeywell

Some principles first

Elements Catalyst Org Model & Impact Analysis

Elements Catalyst runs on AWS with connectors into your Salesforce Org. The managed packaged installed in your Org allows a nightly sync of all your Org metadata – not customer data – into an Org Model.

The Org Model is an easily navigated tree structure, and for each node in the tree we provide useful insights such as Field % Filled and Field Where Used, Field Impact Analysis, links to documentation in the right panel, and the ability to tag items for reporting.

The insights in the right panel or the Org Model can also be visible in Salesforce Setup using a Chrome extension. The right panel is live and fully functional; add documentation, launch process diagrams, post or reply to comments.

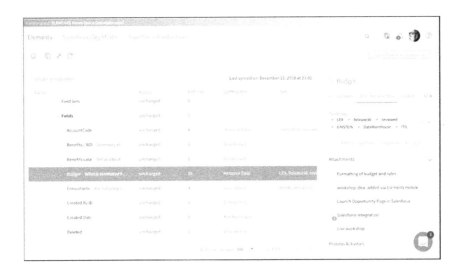

Linking to the Org Model

In the previous chapter we talked about the principles of linking documentation to the Org customizations. Elements Catalyst supports all these link types. It makes is very quick and easy to link to any item in the Org Model.

Linking diagrams (Processes and Data Models)

Link from any process step in a process diagram or entity in a data model to any Org Model item. If the diagrams are drawn in Visio, PowerPoint, Draw.io, Lucidchart or photos of whiteboards, then you have 2 options:

- If the diagram can be accessed via URL - it is a cloud app or has been saved as a PDF and stored in cloud storage - then link the URL (see section below on linking URLs)
- Take a screenshot and attach as an image (see section below on attaching images)

Linking notes

Add a note which can have rich text, either through the web app or using the mobile app.

Linking URL Links in a central library

URL links can be added directly, or the link can be stored in our central URL Links Library to make it easier to link any URL to multiple places. And if the URL destination moves you only have one place to change it – in the library.

Images

Using the web app, you can attach an image or use the camera on your phone and the mobile app. Images are compressed and stored in Elements Catalyst.

Adding metadata

You will want to collect structured metadata via a form. We call this a Data Table. Create a Data Table, attach it to an item in the Org Model and then add data.

Tagging

Any item can have tags so you can report. A tag could be things like delete, reviewed, Release36, marketing, sales.

Linking to Requirements & User Stories

Requirements and user stories that are stored in Elements Catalyst can be linked to any item in the Org Model.

Getting input and collaborating with other teams

Ideally, all comments and collaboration about a particular item should take place in the item's stream rather than in email, Slack, Quip or Chatter because each item in the Org Model has its own stream. The history then stays in context and usually helps fill in the gaps around why things were done a certain way – and who was involved in those discussions.

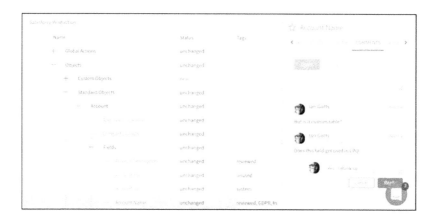

Where to document - Production vs Sandboxes

Each Production and Sandbox is sync'd into a separate Org Model. The Org Models will have some (most) of the same configuration items, but some items only exist in certain Orgs and therefore their related Org Model.

One question is, "Should I link documentation to a Sandbox and what happens when it is deployed to Production?"

This is not an issue. All documentation and comments are held "behind" the Org Models, so no matter which item in Org Model the documentation or comments are added to, they are immediately visible in every other Org Model where that item exists.

That means developers can be adding documentation or commenting to their Sandbox. Trainers could add them to a Sandbox or Production. Business Analysts and Admins could be adding them to Production. And everyone has a view of everything, in real time.

Neat.

It is critical to be able to maintain a single source of truth about the implementation and eliminate conflicts.

Chapter 5: Elements Catalyst

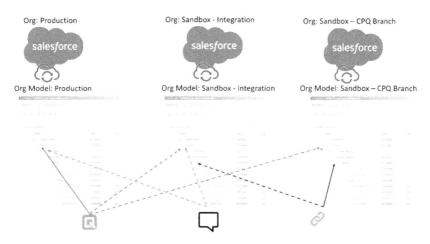

It also means you can run reports to compare Production vs any Sandbox, Sandbox vs Sandbox.

Yes, all of this means work, but it is made easier by having the technology to do the heavy lifting[15].

---

[15] We did explain at the beginning of Chapter 1 that there is no magic bullet. We make it easier to do the right things.

QuickStart Set up & trial

1. Install the Elements Catalyst Managed Package from the AppExchange[16] into the Org you want to sync.
2. Run QuickStart. Helpful video: *http://vimeo.com/286013776*

Quick Start does all the configuration and requires you to confirm the setup in few clicks. It takes just 45 seconds. Quick Start does the following:

- Creates an Elements Catalyst user account where the user name is your email address associated with Salesforce username (not your Salesforce username2)
- Creates a new Space called "Salesforce Documentation" and makes it a Pro Trial - 14 days, 3 Editors
- Makes the connections between Salesforce and Elements in both directions

Finally, you kick off the initial sync to the Org. This is only your core metadata, not any customer data.

When sync has finished (Org Model has been built and the impact analysis has been completed), you will get an email. Yay!!

That email will have a link to open the Org Model and also a link to the Org Analytics Report.

---

[16] *https://appexchange.salesforce.com/appxListingDetail?listingId=a0N3A00000EIicYUAT*

Architecture

Org Model principles

The tree structure is called an Org Model. Each Org Model is sync'd from an Org (Production or Sandbox) and the metadata is held in our database in AWS. We do not access your data, only your metadata. We use the Metadata and Tools APIs to get the metadata.

You can set up a nightly sync of the Org Model. After every sync you will be sent an email of the metadata items that have been added or changed since the sync. This is useful if you have multiple Admins or managed packages which are being updated and are changing both their custom objects and the standard objects.

The connector does not use a Salesforce license.

Production vs Sandbox

You can sync Production and Sandbox Orgs. Each will be linked to a separate Org Model.

Access and security

Only you can see the Org Models until you give a user access as an Editor or Viewer.

Editors and Viewers do not have to be Salesforce Users, but there is Single Sign On for Salesforce as part of the Managed Package.

Elements Catalyst Usernames vs Salesforce Usernames

Think of a Space like a Salesforce Implementation. The Elements Catalyst and Salesforce username structure are slightly different. We wanted to make it easier to manage multiple Spaces and Orgs - from a single user login - so we didn't copy the Salesforce approach.

First, we need to understand the naming conventions.

Salesforce user name

- A username is linked to an individual Org - a Dev, Production or a Sandbox Org. You cannot have the same username to log into multiple Orgs.
- It is a random name but it needs to be in an email format e.g. *name@name.name*
- Pick a naming convention that is easy to remember quick to type. The shortest you are allowed is *a@a.aa*
- Every username has an email address associated with it. Multiple usernames can have the same email address.
- Username needs to be unique across ALL Salesforce users everywhere:

Username	Email	Org
another.devorg@1.prod	pete@zenalpha.com	Production
sandbox1@za.za	pete@zenalpha.com	Sandbox-CPQ
pete@123.com.sandbox	pete@zenalpha.com	Sandbox-int
pete@123.com.sandbox.cons	pete@zenalpha.com	Sandbox-cons
dev123.pete@test.aa	pete@zenalpha.com	Dev123

Elements Catalyst user names

Your email address. A real email address. *pete@zenalpha.com*

You log into Elements Catalyst - there is only one instance.

An Elements Catalyst user can access **multiple** Spaces.

Elements Catalyst Spaces

- A Space is a secure, ring-fenced work area. Think of it as an "implementation of Elements"
- DO NOT think of Spaces as folders. A corporate will probably only have ONE Space. A consulting firm will have one Space for internal operations and a separate one for every client
- You can invite users to Spaces. They can then only see what is in that Space - provided they have been given view or edit rights. Every user in a Space can see the other users
- An Elements Catalyst user can be a member of multiple Spaces. One login - multiple Spaces
- Whoever sets up the Space is the Admin. But you can assign admin rights to multiple people and Admin rights can be transferred by assigning admin rights to another, who then removes yours. A Space could be set up by a consultant and then transferred to the client at the end of the project
- A user needs a separate license for each Space they are an Editor in
- A Space can be FREE, PRO, PRO-TRIAL, ENTERPRISE or UNLIMITED

Here is the important part.....

Each Salesforce Org is sync'd to its Elements Catalyst Org Model.

A Space can be connected to multiple Salesforce Orgs (Production & Sandbox). So a Space will have multiple Org Models.

This image shows how multiple Salesforce Orgs can be sync'd to Elements Catalyst Spaces.

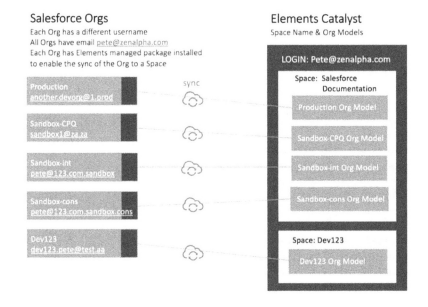

Logging in and accessing the Org Model

With OAuth in Salesforce you can log in using your Elements Catalyst user name (your email associated with Salesforce login) and if you click on LOGIN SALESFORCE then you will use your Salesforce credentials and Elements will use the password stored in Salesforce.

Giving others access to the Org Model

You are the Admin of the Salesforce Documentation Space and the manager of the Org Models you have sync'd with your Org. Now you can give co-workers and consultants access to the Org Model and process maps so that they can view them, add comments or documentation.

Viewers, who are free, can view and add comments to the Org Model and process diagrams.

Editors, who need a license, can do everything a Viewer can PLUS they can add documentation, draw process diagrams, and add links. They can progress a requirement from "submitted" though the lifecycle to "closed".

The important thing is that Editor and Viewer licenses do not need a Salesforce license and it doesn't matter how many users you have in your Salesforce Orgs. You will simply need a Salesforce Administrator to install the managed package and to set up sync using QuickStart or manual setup. In practice, we find that each Admin and Business Analyst will need an Editor license.

Chapter 6: Org Impact Analysis

The Elements Catalyst Org Model provides powerful org analysis right out-of-the-box for core metadata and your managed packages. And it does the analysis every time you sync. The sync uses the Tools and Metadata APIs. You can automate the sync to run nightly.

The tree structure of the Org Model may be the first time you've seen a perspective of your Org like this. The reaction may be "WOW", "OMG" or "Ahhh, that's why…" How big is your Org? We'll give you a summary on the right panel[17].

There is also an Elements Catalyst Salesforce Org Analytics report that runs on the Org Model data.

---

[17] It may feel a little like rubbernecking at the accident on the other side of the freeway. But go ahead. No-one else is watching!

Chapter 6: Org Impact Analysis

You can click on the Launch Salesforce Org Analytics report button in the toolbar of the Org Model. The Org Analytics report opens up in a new tab in the browser and can be run at any time as it builds the report from the latest Org Model data.

Take a quick look at the contents on the left panel of the Org Analytics report to see what is currently provided. Click on any item in the contents to go to that section. The report is interactive. You can filter and sort the graphs. This is more detailed than Salesforce Optimizer but is very much focused on the configuration of your Org and how well documented it is.

The analysis in the Org Model and the Org Analytics report has been designed to help you focus your efforts on clean-up and documentation. It reduces the detective and analysis work for you.

Navigating the Org Model tree structure

Let's go back to the Org Model in the other tab and start to drill into the Org Model. You can see that it is a tree structure and if you click on the arrow alongside any item (we call them nodes) you can expand it to see the next level of detail (child nodes) and so on down multiple levels.

The node has the name of the customization (e.g. the Object name) and in italics the description field is pulled from Salesforce, if a description field exists for that type of customization. Not everything in Salesforce has a description field, such as Apex Classes or Lightning pages. The columns - Tags, Status, GDPR, # of links - can be dragged to change position and size. You can automate the sync to run nightly. If an item in Salesforce is deleted, then the next time the sync runs, the Org Model shows the Status as deleted but keeps it in the tree structure along with any documentation you may have linked to it.

The Org Model right panel

Click on the top level of the Org Model (the top row of the tree "Salesforce Production") and the right panel gives you an overview of all customizations in both the core and managed packages. The right panel scrolls so you can see more information. If you click on the SYNC HISTORY tab you can see the history of the previous syncs but you can also kick off a new sync from here.

Then you can start opening up the tree structure to drill into lower levels. Keep an eye on the right panel, as we provide you information on the item you selected. Every item has the DETAILS, LINKS and COMMENTS tabs. But some metadata types like Objects, Fields, Dashboards and Reports have more tabs.

DETAILS tab has the information that is available through the Salesforce APIs. It varies for each type of node in the Org Model. There is also a link to open up that customization in Salesforce Setup if a setup page exists for it.

DOCUMENTATION tab is where you can add documentation. This can be notes, URL links, Data Tables (metadata on metadata), process diagrams and requirements.

COMMENTS is like a Chatter stream for every node where you can @mention colleagues. Again, the free Viewer licenses allow posting comments.

Managed Packages

All metadata from managed packages are sync'd. The custom metadata is under the Managed Packages section. Managed Packages also add nodes to standard objects such as fields, page layouts. These are found in the core objects section.

Objects

In the Objects section there will be a Standard Objects section and if you have custom objects then there will be a Custom Objects section.

Click on an Object and the right panel gives a summary of the object including the number of records by record type. Just keep scrolling down the right panel to see the analysis.

Objects have an additional tab USAGE. This shows which fields (system, standard, custom) have data in them. Remember all those custom fields that were asked for? Now you can see if they were even used.

Click on USAGE and then filter the fields by Custom.

Fields

Fields have several additional tabs:

USAGE shows how populated fields are by record type and also where fields are used. The analysis covers email templates, page layouts, reports, automation and rules.

ACCESS tab shows the field access by user for permission sets and profiles. This needs to be requested on demand as it is a huge analysis task. That's why it is not done for every field in every object every time the sync is run. There is a link in the tab to kick off the analysis and collect the data which is done asynchronously.

GDPR collects the data required for GDPR compliance.

The USAGE and ACCESS analysis would be impossible to do manually and keep up-to-date.

Finally, you will see that every item has a Salesforce Setup icon. This will open Salesforce in Setup page for that item, saving you endless clicks navigating through Setup.

When you are in Setup, if you have the Chrome Extension installed you can access all the insights and documentation from the Org Model in the right panel.

By default, Setup will open up in Classic, but you can change it to open up in Lightning. The setting is in the Elements Catalyst Space Management page in the Connections section. You will recognize the page as this is where you agreed to the authentications during QuickStart. This is also where you can set up nightly syncs and manually kick off a sync.

Chapter 7: Developing great documentation habits

There is no later

The quickest and easiest time to add documentation is "in the moment". It is fresh in your mind, you remember the rationale and you have the item open on screen.

Nike said it best back in 1988. "Just Do It".

Think of this as a tweet to say "Wow – look what I've just created". A quick 280 characters or photo that will be gold dust in 6 months' time.

Take the example of a validation rule. 30 mins to build, validate and test. It could take 2 hours to work that out 3 months later. Adding documentation takes 5 minutes, max. BTW It could be even faster if you created a process diagram to understand the process that needed the validation. Then it is 30 seconds to connect the process diagram to the validation. No need to create extra documentation.

At a minimum, fill out the descriptions in Salesforce. Did you know that you can update descriptions and help text directly from the Elements Catalyst Org Model?

Working where you work

We started looking at where you as Admins, Developers and Consultants work: in Salesforce Setup, in your development IDE, in workshops with users, inside Quip, and in the Org Model. That's where we needed to make it easy for you to add documentation. We wanted to take away the friction and excuses.

That's why we created the Chrome extension to provide the Org Model inside Salesforce Setup. We developed the mobile app. The Quip Live App is in security review.

We also looked at the principles of Chatter and wanted the discussions about configuration out of email and into the app. So, every item in the Org Model has its own discussion stream.

Finally, you don't need to be a Salesforce user to edit, collaborate on or view the Org Model. Anyone can be invited in to collaborate and contribute[18].

---

[18] The more the merrier – "the sales team"

Chapter 8: Lightning Migration

Migrating to Lightning

Salesforce is investing a huge amount of time and effort into Lightning enhancements and encouraging customers to migrate. Salesforce's R&D investments are in Lightning – currently 840 Lightning experience-only features.

The migration to Lightning gives you an opportunity to take advantage of the changes that Salesforce has made to ensure that users get their work done faster and more efficiently than ever.

With the new features you can redesign leaner operational processes and get the huge benefits you see other customers are talking about. Delete unused Managed Packages saving license fees. Eliminate code and messy workarounds using the new powerful automation tools like Flow and Process Builder Workflow.

Use it as the opportunity to make a new, fresh start.

31% less time managing pipe and 28% less time standardizing processes, with 21% uplift in win rates, 29% faster reporting, 40% improved collaboration, and 41% higher productivity

Salesforce on Salesforce, A Lightning Story

Chapter 8: Lightning Migration

The migration forces you to get a good understanding of how your Org works and to look for ways to clean up and optimize it. But it is difficult to optimize and simplify if your view of the current business processes and related customizations is hazy.

As we've discussed previously in this book, the project might seem too big to tackle, as you don't have a clear view of everything in your Org and how it all connects.

You need to work through all the items that need fixing and then decide how your users experience could be transformed. But that means changes to page layouts and validation rules and workflows etc. Getting a grip on how and why these customizations were made is a vital first step.

Using Lightning Experience Readiness report and the Elements Catalyst Org Analytics report you can see where to focus your clean-up efforts to get some quick wins.

The Org Model analytics and reporting eliminates man weeks of tedious analysis.

Document what you have discovered and build an estimate of the effort to migrate in the Org Model.

As you build your new Lightning experience you have a place to start documenting what and why. I know we keep saying this, but – make documentation a habit.

Let's look at the migration project in more detail.

Lighting Rollout

The Rollout Lightning Experience planning document[19] has some really valuable advice as you start to look at migration. The approach in this book dovetails with the Salesforce Lightning Experience Rollout planning methodology, which has three phases: Discover, Rollout and Optimize. We'll cover each one in turn.

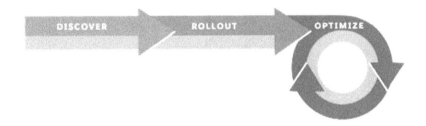

DISCOVER

You need a quick and efficient Discover phase to kick off your migration project. The first 4 activities in the Discover phase are:

- Identify Stakeholders and an Executive Sponsor
- Revisit Your Processes
- Perform Gap Analysis
- Optimize your Implementation

Let's look at how Elements Catalyst[20] can help accelerate these steps.

---

[19] Rollout Lightning Experience to your company *http://bit.ly/2yWcSyG*
[20] Maybe we should have called it Elements CSI rather than Elements Catalyst

Identify Stakeholders and an Executive Sponsor

Do you even know which users are most active in Salesforce – by permission set or profile? The Elements Catalyst Org Analysis report will give you a better picture of the activity of the user base. You need to identify the user representatives from each business area that you want to work on the project.

Revisit Your Processes

Some great advice from the Lighting Experience Rollout planning document[21]; "Ask directly, 'Can we change the way we do it?' The value proposition of new, improved functionality might be worth updating an existing process."

The fastest and most engaging approach is live process mapping workshops with your stakeholders, representatives and executive sponsor. Not only do you get shared agreement on the new processes, but you are also starting the change management process. You will identify quick wins that don't require any changes to Salesforce. BTW This is the HOW.

The first step on this Lightning Experience journey was reassessing the processes that we had and the personas that we were delivering experiences for, making sure that what they had in Salesforce Classic was focused on what was going to make them successful.

Tacy Parker, GTM Business Architecture, Salesforce

---

[21] Rollout Lightning Experience to your company *http://bit.ly/2vWcSvG*

We have years of experience of running live process mapping workshops. That experience is distilled into a guide in Appendix 2.

Elements is just so easy to use. Any Salesforce Admin should be able to pick it up and be able to start mapping in live workshops really quickly.

Benjamin Bolopue, Salesforce CRM Administrator, MVP,

Quanex Building Products

Perform Gap Analysis

Once you run the Lightning Experience Readiness Check it will identify what you need to change. You can match this against the redesigned business processes to see if those changes even need to be made.

This is the WHAT and the WHY.

Then you can work through the process diagrams, step-by-step, and work out what in Salesforce (objects, fields, automation, email templates, Apex triggers and classes, reports etc.) needs to be migrated.

You can also see which Managed Packages you still need to keep and delete those that are not required.

At the same time you can start tracking the effort and risk required to make any changes to migrate any item. This can be tracked in an Elements Catalyst Data Table[22], so you can run a report to give you an overall picture of the effort and risks. You can also use tagging to highlight items in the Org Model that are going to be migrated so you can report, but also get a visual as you scan down the Org Model.

Improve your implementation (and avoid conflicts)

This is essentially your clean-up project. You have already started this work as you revisited your business processes (HOW) and performed your gap analysis (WHAT & WHY).

The Rollout Lightning Experience planning document recommends using Salesforce Optimizer, which gives a broad overview of the health of your Org. But Elements Catalyst provides more in-depth analysis for optimizing and documenting your Org[23]. It can save you man-months of tedious work combing through Setup to establish relationships and field usage and field impact. You will identify migration conflicts. If you are moving to Lightning using a phased approach – different groups of users e.g. Partner Managements vs Sales Operations – you may discover that certain customizations are used by multiple groups who are migrating to Lightning at different times. Those customizations will need to work in both Lightning and Classic until everybody has migrated. It is far better to discover this issue now, rather than post-implementation.

How would you see this? If you start connecting the process activities for each group to the Salesforce customizations you will see which are used by both groups and therefore spot the conflict.

---

[22] Using Data Tables *http://bit.ly/elementsLEX*
[23] We'd LOVE Salesforce to recommend us for Lightning migrations. We're working on it!!!

Getting Hands-on with Lightning Experience

Lightning Experience is now so broad, that this effort needs to be directed. You cannot possibly look at all functionality[24]. Instead, focus your discover phase around the redesigned processes and the potential Lightning functionality that can be used to improve the user experience.

Educate your company about the Lightning Experience

As the Lightning Experience Rollout planning document highlights - one of the most important questions your executive sponsor and stakeholders will have is, "How will Lightning Experience help my team sell more?" .

This question can only be answered in the context of the new business processes which they will have been involved in developing.

---

[24] The Spring19 Release Note is 457 pages
https://resources.docs.salesforce.com/218/latest/en-us/sfdc/pdf/salesforce_spring19_release_notes.pdf

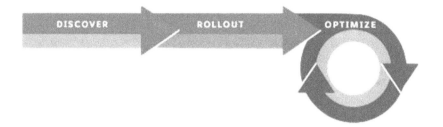

ROLLOUT

Plan your Rollout

The discovery work needs to inform your planning. How much effort? What is the risk? How should it be phased? What is driving the changes?

Companies that survive and thrive on change tend to follow a familiar pattern:

- First of all, everyone involved understands that change happens and things need to change.
- Secondly, there is someone clearly leading and driving the strategy. Everyone buys into the change and understands the critical reasons it needs to happen. The company is actually capable of change; the capability and ability to change, learn and innovate over time.
- And finally and most importantly, it does not happen overnight. There is no such thing as 'instant change.'

Successful change management is stubborn, persistent and consistent.

There are 4 different strategies to change which are described in an article I'll summarize on the next page – 4 Change Strategies7. You need to decide which suits your company culture, maturity and the market conditions.

4 Strategies for Implementing Change

FACTOR

Speed: How important is speed to accomplishing the objectives of the change effort? Is the pace determined by the markets, the competition or the customers?

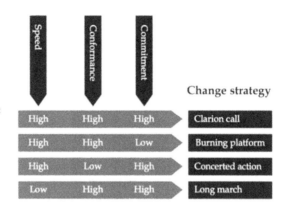

Speed	Conformance	Commitment	Change strategy
High	High	High	Clarion call
High	High	Low	Burning platform
High	Low	High	Concerted action
Low	High	High	Long march

Conformance:
How closely must we follow the specific processes or outcome to achieve our goals? Is there regulatory pressure to conform, or would it stifle innovation?

Commitment: How important is it to ensure that everyone in the negotiation understands the need for change and is prepared to do what it takes?

STRATEGY

Clarion call: This strategy requires that the change is driven by senior management leadership who show a strong commitment to the change. This is because the need and needed speed for change are not apparent further down the organization.

Burning platform: Everyone already recognizes the need for change. Therefore, a clear message about what is required in order to implement change is needed. The risk is that the actions from different parts of the organization (in their panic) are uncoordinated and inconsistent.

Concerted action: This requires delegation of the change so that it can be applied autonomously throughout the organization. Yet it still requires the changes to fit within the overall business strategy.

Long march: A long-term initiative which has a strong identity and clear sponsorship from the top so that there is continued commitment to the change. No-one loses sight of the end goal. It also requires clear metrics to show that the changes are working.

Develop and test (AND DOCUMENT)²⁵ customizations

Migrating to Lightning is not necessarily just switching a switch. Reading Salesforce's own migration story is illuminating.

Here are some of the stats:

- 60 managed packages
- 1,752 VisualForce pages
- 438 updated Visualforce pages
- 177 updated reports
- 145 Javascript links and buttons converted
- 23 citizen-developed custom apps outside scope of IT Team

Your Org may not be as big and scary, but there will inevitably be changes to make. And you'll need to build new Lightning Pages to exploit the new features.

Now is the chance to strengthen those new documentation habits, building on the documentation you've already created through the DISCOVER phase.

Remember. There is no "Later". Document the changes as you go.

---

²⁵ Can you spot which extra activity we added

Rollout and training

Change is hard. You need to support your users as they start to use the new UI. You also want them to discover and use the new features that will make them more efficient. Human nature shows that they will revert to old working practices, using Salesforce just as they did with Classic, with a prettier UI. That would be wasting the effort it took to migrate.

Remember those process maps you developed? They can be used as training material embedded inside Salesforce Lightning pages or the Utility Bar. Or develop other training material in Elements Catalyst that is more geared to the user experience you want. You don't just have to draw boring processes. Diagrams can have images, text and hotspots to launch training videos. And it is all version controlled and managed inside Elements Catalyst.

Don't assume implementation leads to adoption. Not only do you have to think about all the steps in implementing Lightning Experience, but also all of the change management.

Michael Gonella, CIO, Salesforce

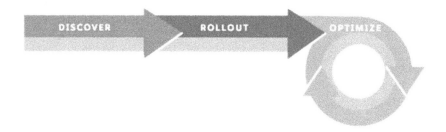

OPTIMIZE

In the Rollout phase you identified some success metrics. You can start to measure your adoption against those metrics and iterate.

Iteration is SO MUCH FASTER when you have a clear view about what was configured, and why: the documentation. The impact analysis enables you to reduce the risks of making changes in one area which affect other areas.

Some changes may be tweaks to Lightning page layouts to improve the user experience and readability. Other changes may be more significant such as business process improvements. In which case you need to go back to the business process diagrams and start there. That way you make sure that it all hangs together, and if the process diagrams are used as training material, they will be automatically updated when published.

And whatever you change. Document it.

Chapter 9: The Director's Cut

Why you need to implement CRM twice

There is a great eBook that Accenture has written called The Director's Cut[26]. The thrust behind it is:

How do movie directors create new value with their previously released films? They issue a "director's cut"— a revised, updated version of a previously released movie over which the director has complete artistic control. In issuing an original film, directors battle against deadlines, budgets, resource constraints and movie studio executives who sometimes demand a different product than the director's original vision. But with the advent of new technologies, new marketing opportunities and newly available funds and resources, a director has the opportunity to revisit his original idea and deliver a new and stronger film.

How does this apply to Salesforce? For many implementations, the first project is the struggle to configure, build integrations and convert data. Engaging end users, redesigning processes, training and driving adoption are all chopped out of the plan in the scramble to go live within budget. The second attempt at the implementation - The Director's Cut - addresses all these softer factors.

The eBook is beautifully written. What is surprising is that it was written in 2002.

But the idea is very relevant to your Lightning migration project. This is your chance to "re-implement Salesforce"; starting again for the first time.

---

[26] _http://bit.ly/accenturedc_

The only difference that I can see between 2002 and now is that the apps are in the cloud. Cloud eliminates the hardware procurement and software installation. Everything else you would have found in Accenture's 2002 project plan is still required.

In fact, I dusted off the Andersen Consulting (Accenture) Method/1 implementation methodology for Packaged Systems Selection & Design and Packaged Systems Installation – dated 1992. Of the 17 major work packages, ONLY ONE can be eliminated because of the cloud - "Hardware and software installation".

So why are we still failing to drive a tangible ROI first time, on time, on budget? And how can we learn from this for our Lightning migration?

First, don't buy the "just switch it on" line. Migrations that are going to deliver real benefits are still going to need to change the hearts and minds of a large number of people. Marketing, sales admin, inside sales, field sales and management will all need to work slightly differently, using the better UI.

Second, take a process driven approach. Document business processes with users to help them get a really clear understanding of their requirements. This will ensure that the customizations you build hang together to support the end-to-end processes including the handoffs.

The biggest CRM failure reason I've seen is companies trying to implement CRM software without alignment to customer strategy or regard for changes in business processes. These companies seem to believe that the CRM software in itself will benefit the company. In reality, this approach can add value in terms of record keeping, data management and some information visibility, but it will certainly not increase customer relationships.

A problem we incurred when trying to implement our Salesforce.com CRM system was not recognizing and fixing our inefficient and broken business processes before we deployed the new system. Only after we realized we were implementing far less than ideal business processes in the new CRM software did we stop the effort. This caused us to terminate a 3-month implementation, go back and revise processes and then start again. We eventually got it right, but that lesson learned cost us an extra 6 months.

Chapter 9: The Director's Cut

Chapter 10: Keeping on top of your Org

You've worked hard to get your Org cleaned up and documented. How do keep it that way without killing the creativity and agility of the development cycle?

You need to get a robust but agile change management process in place. This chapter looks at how you can embed some of the documentation principles into the Development Lifecycle, without making it a huge administrative burden.

Process for process improvement

Below is a process map called Salesforce Development Lifecycle which has lower level diagrams with more detail and useful links (paperclip). It is available to be copied from the "Example process maps" Public Space. We will continue to develop it with more useful resources.

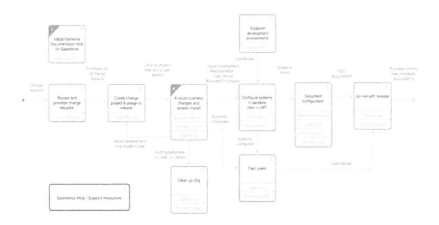

Impact Analysis

One critical new activity is box 4, Impact Analysis. Previously, you probably didn't have the data or tools to do any real impact analysis of changes. Now you have. This will speed up the pace of change. It will improve your confidence to make changes, reduce risk and increase the agility of the business.

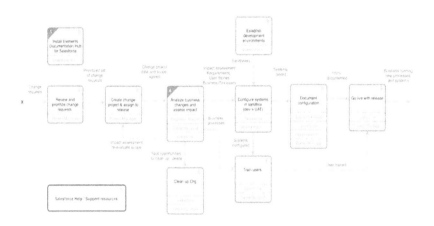

Documentation audit

The Elements Catalyst Salesforce Org Analysis report will give tell you how well changes are documented – as descriptions in Salesforce and as attached documentation, processes and requirements in the Org Model.

We have one client who said, "No change goes live into Production until the documentation is at 100% in the Org Model".

Appendix 1: resources

General Resources

- Analysis, Automation and Adoption eBook -
  http://bit.ly/AnalysisAutoandAdop

Training on HOW. WHAT. WHY Approach

- Catalyst Trail for Clean-up and Documentation –
  http://bit.ly/cleanuptrail
- Catalyst Trail for User Adoption – *http://bit.ly/adoptiontrail*
- Catalyst Trail for Consultants. – *http://bit.ly/consultingtrail*
- How to draw map processes/draw diagrams -
  http://bit.ly/howtoelements
- Trailhead Superbadge - *http://bit.ly/superbadge*

Links in book

Chapter 2

- Forrester report summary: Five ways to cut the risk of
  Salesforce - *https://www.computerweekly.com/feature/Five-ways-to-cut-the-risk-of-Salesforce*

Chapter 3

- Lightning Readiness Check Overview –
  https://sforce.co/2D3rf8W

Chapter 4

- 7-minute exercise routine - *https://7-min.com/*
- Business process mapping principles - *http://bit.ly/processmapping*
- David Limiero podcast about consolidating processes - *http://bit.ly/stadiachurchplanting*

Chapter 5

- App Exchange for installing Catalyst App - *https://appexchange.salesforce.com/appxListingDetail?listingId=a0 N3A00000EJicYUAT*
- Running Quickstart video - *https://vimeo.com/286013776*

Chapter 8

- Rollout Lightning Experience to your company - *http://bit.ly/2yWcSyG*
- Using Data Tables - *http://bit.ly/elementsLEX*
- Spring 19 Release Notes - *https://resources.docs.salesforce.com/218/latest/en-us/sfdc/pdf/salesforce_spring19_release_notes.pdf*
- 4 Strategies for Implementing Change - *http://bit.ly/4changestrategies*

Chapter 9

- The Director's Cut eBook - *http://bit.ly/accenturedc*

Appendix 2: Running Live Workshops

Live process mapping

Using live workshops to map out business processes is far more effective than completing questionnaires or conducting individual interviews. Whilst live workshops - either face to face or virtual - seem scary and high risk, the benefits are huge.

Don't underestimate how much time this saves, or the value delivered for the time expended. It will take far less time than you think to become proficient at running live mapping workshops. To start with, you may feel more comfortable with 2 facilitators; one to "work the room" and one to use Elements Catalyst to map the processes. It has been designed to work really well in live workshops, whether face to face or virtual.

Benefits of LIVE workshops

- They build consensus in the group and rapidly drive out improvement ideas. Some of these ideas are quick wins that don't even need Salesforce changes

- You are developing the process content in the workshop, so there's no need to try and interpret notes or photos of whiteboards when you get back to your desk to build the process diagrams.

- It is easier to get agreement and sign-off when the participants see it being developed and they have had input as it is being created.

Workshop principles

- 5P's = Preparation Prevents Particularly Poor Performance. This about the likely process you are developing, the politics in the room, the objections...
- The important thing is to get interaction and momentum. Get them talking/arguing. It may start slowly, but it is worth investing the time to build consensus.
- Before you do anything, EXPLAIN HOW you are going to capture the process i.e. use the WHAT WHY and HOW diagram. Show the use of the verb and noun construct. Show then an example of a completed map with activity boxes, resources, attachments and drilldowns.
- Map using Elements.cloud Catalyst app.
- Do not opt out and just use a whiteboard for the mapping – ok for higher level objectives and notes – but these should all end up in the Map in appropriate places and contexts.
- Spend time to be clear on the outcomes that the end-to-end process covered by this workshop is looking to deliver. Use the sticky notes to put these key outcomes on the screen so you can move them around. If you're all in the same room, a whiteboard is also great.
- Set the scope of the workshop by looking at the first input and last output. It may take a surprisingly long time to get agreement on this. YOU CANNOT move forward until this is agreed.
- To get them to focus on activities use "I have just joined your organization as a XXXX, and I need to XXX. How do I know what to do next? How do I know when I've finished?"
- Map the "assume it works" flow. Do not get bogged down into all the exceptions and variations until you have mapped the "assume it works" route (what happens most often) end-to-end.
- Check regularly with the participants that the mapped information is an accurate representation of what was discussed. If they can't agree, move to a whiteboard to sketch a flow of processes, then go back and map.

Preparation

- Scope of project from project proposal and scope document
- Objectives of overall project (key business outcomes that this project contributes to)
- Objective of workshop from project sponsor, project manager and Salesforce Admin
- Personal objectives of project sponsor, project manager and Salesforce Admin
- Scope & context of workshop - input and output
- Audience – name, role, title
- What personal conflicts & politics in the group, and where is power?
- Terminology – what will turn them on, turn them off, no-no's
- How much understanding & buy-in does the audience have of processes?
- What is the pain to resolve?
- Where is ROI or win?

Agenda

- Introductions – go around the room
- Introduce session – why they are there, pain, …
- Objectives of the session – working meeting to get a result
- Benefits of session
    - defines company operational strategy
    - sets context for specific projects
    - sets priorities for improvement projects
    - kick start projects
- Project sponsor demonstrates support
- Show 'finished product' process diagram so they know what they are aiming a
- Strategic objectives on white board (tangible – with measures)
- Map processes

- Identify Salesforce configuration
- Identify supporting information or link to known information directly
- Identify process owners
- Identify metrics
- Identify priority processes for initial projects
- Next steps

Approach

- Optimum duration for each process mapping session should be no more than 3-4 hours. People start losing interest after that.
- Keep participants to between 8-10 people (Process Owner, Key Stakeholders, SMEs). They need to understand that they will be required to participate NOT observe.
- It is strongly recommended that the facilitator should be different from the process mapper. Especially in large workshops the mapper will be too busy capturing to facilitate properly. Clearly the exception is where you are driving a group remotely. In either case, ensure the person doing the mapping is reasonably quick with a keyboard and mouse and familiar with Elements Catalyst. It is very quick, but you don't want to learn about it with an audience!
- It is useful if the facilitator is not an expert in the field being discussed – allows them to ask the 'obvious' questions, point out glaring inconsistencies, and prevents them from steering the group towards the facilitator's personal preferences.
- With remote sessions, ensure people are on the same diagram in Elements Catalyst and understand how to add comments to contribute remotely. Doing this direct in the Elements Catalyst means all threads are maintained in the context of the diagram, instead of lost at the end of the web session or detached in an unrelated chatter stream.
- Get people involved. If you are remote, encourage interruption and comments, use sticky notes to capture people's input. You can always stack them up for resolution later or move them out of the currently visible area.

- If you're in the same location, don't be afraid to use white boards and Post-It notes, but make sure you capture them all at the end of the session in the context of the diagram.

Ground Rules

- Focus on the "assume it works" process first. Then map out exceptions.
- Silence = Agreement
- Park/board unresolved issues after 5 minutes of discussion.
- Map out processes one level at a time starting at the highest level THEN drill down into more and more details (i.e., Inputs, Activities, Outputs, Resources). Wherever possible, outputs should not be the past tense of the Activity, but should add value to the process description.
- Keep diagrams readable (8-10 activity boxes per diagram). One conversation at a time.
- Map activities NOT functions!
- All participants are equal, and everyone's input is welcome. Managers – do not dominate the discussion – let the people who actually do it have their say.

Appendix 2: Running Live Workshops

Notes pages

We hope that this book has inspired you and that you have already scribbled your thoughts all over it. However, if you have ideas that need a little more space then please use these notes pages.

Notes pages

www.ingramcontent.com/pod-product-compliance
Lightning Source LLC
LaVergne TN